CW01501719

ABOUT THE AUTHOR

Hayley Frances is a poet from Birmingham. Her work explores the psychology of creative writing and its use as a therapeutic medium. In 2024 she was appointed the first Poet in Residence for Birmingham Women's and Children's Hospital. *Administer the Laughing Gas* is her debut collection.

Hayley Frances
Administer the Laughing Gas

VERVE
POETRY PRESS
BIRMINGHAM

PUBLISHED BY VERVE POETRY PRESS
https://vervepoetrypress.com
mail@vervepoetrypress.com

All rights reserved
© 2024 Hayley Frances

The right of Hayley Frances to be identified as author of this work has
been asserted in accordance with section 77 of the Copyright, Designs and
Patents Act 1988.

No part of this work may be reproduced, stored or transmitted in any form
or by any means, graphic, electronic, recorded or mechanical, without the
prior written permission of the publisher.

FIRST PUBLISHED SEP 2024

Printed and bound in the UK
by ImprintDigital, Exeter

ISBN: 978-1-913917-54-8

For the midwives

CONTENTS

Introduction

Acknowledgements

INTRODUCTION

This book wasn't written for you. I didn't intend for it to happen. The poems that initiated this collection were selected as the only poems I had out of all the poems I'd written that had potential. The recurring theme between the selected poems at the time was my attempt at translating grief after going into early labour and losing my daughter. I intentionally sent a ton of poems to a publishing friend to avoid overwhelming him with that experience. He, unintentionally, pulled out the ones associated with her, and here she is, unintentionally arriving in your hands like she unintentionally arrived in our life.

These poems were written in silence and isolation. What happened to me was a burden, a sadness too dark to talk about. The only place I felt safe to elicit her existence and the intense emptiness within was through poetry. I wanted so much for her to be real rather than this awful circumstance. I wanted her to be more than the silent trauma she was within the secrets of a hospital. I also wanted to be a mom. It occurred to me in the editing of this collection that the isolate, intimate act of writing poetry mirrored the isolate, intimate act of early motherhood. I tended to my grief like a mom tends to a newborn. These poems were a way for me to feel what I could not touch, hold who didn't survive, keep me company in the sleepless nights my body had prepared itself for post-birth, and feed the part of me that I couldn't with the milk I'd made. They weren't written to be read.

Writing is a solitary act. It weaves together the material and spiritual, the emotional and logical. It translates experiences through symbolism, imagery and metaphor, and contains what we struggle to understand or communicate within the poem. It allows you to be ethereal, confused, sad, loving and overwhelmed. Poetry desires the depths of human emotion - as Billy Collins put it - "poetry is the greatest historian of the human heart".

In a sense, this book has taken 8 years to write. Even though writing's a place of solace for me, it's also a place of pain, and often, I've procrastinated on this collection out of fear of revisiting what happened or retranslating myself. Whenever I relinquish myself to that fear, I've found something new in the poems, and subsequently, formed a deeper relationship with myself. This book then also faces fear. What you'll find isn't a series of sonnets or limericks or couplets. I haven't manipulated my expression to adhere to those standards. Each poem is me or her or both of us or midwives or women or daughters or parents or love or grief or consciousness. It's awareness making itself aware through me. It's a witness making my experiences more than a memory.

Grief is unwavering like that. She shows up in almost everything, even though she was barely here. After birth, she showed me the fragility of human existence. She showed me motherhood through my loss of it. She showed me the lengths we go to to keep an idea alive. She showed me you can grieve a future that hasn't materialised, and how often we lose ourselves in chasing imaginary futures. I didn't leave it alone; I wanted to understand the spirit, how it comes into being, where it goes after life, where emotions are born, how they affect the body and what even is a soul anyway?

This book is a witness. I sourced the sight of awareness through poetry. The poems in this book opened me up in a way only a dedication to scrutinising grief can. Had I have 'gotten on' with life without witnessing grief and trying to understand it, I would be a shadow of the woman I have become. This book is my way of remembering, it's her living within and beside me. That's what this book is. It honours human form, and the need to grieve, and the need to express grief. This book is not written for your entertainment. It is not written to please you. It is not here to satisfy. It isn't an example of poetry therapy. It isn't proof I can write. It isn't a right of passage. It's me trying to find myself, attempting to make real what I feel and imagine, what we went through and the impact of that.

This book wasn't written for you. When I tried to make this book for you, it lost me, and I lost myself, which is funny because this book is about loss. I had to lose so much for this book to be, and this is the final loss, letting it go, letting it fly into your hands - each side in each palm a wing. This book is an angel then, or a bird that wants to fly away. It's a symbol of love, loss and homecoming and, therefore, will never be finished.

I've written a wound you can open with your fingers that's healing with every poem you read.

Hayley Frances, 2024

Administer the Laughing Gas

Blessed art thou among women, and blessed is the fruit of thy womb

I try to digest
the whole apple tree,
it always comes up in pieces.
It can't seed in my core,
it can't satisfy
the men in there who
churn business.

Petal lids

'I want to call her closed lids
buds because shut
they look like petals
tucked away which could
at any moment bud'.
                    - Will Harris.

I,
a conjecture of want,
didn't know I'd need her eyes to
see my sight until they couldn't open. Call
it reflection if you want, but it's self-witness. In her
the daughters immature mirrors fuzed closed.
If the veil of her lids
were buds,
her eyes would have refracted a sense of girlhood because
as my Sun, she would light me into rising song. Shut,
she never saw her image in mine either. If they
who are us not observed in our look,
do they live? This book is our gaze. She is present, like
petals
that pierce colour tucked
into green and fall when bees take pollen away
and crisp to dust before dirt before earth and which
dry up in the home but stay as a memory that could
become an awakening. It's natures fierce happening at
once, arriving and parting, planting and weeding any
imperfection to protect the view of each moment
and give a thing that needs some air a chance to bud.

JOURNEY #1

She was born late enough for saving but too early in her development for her eyes to open. How was I to know our root to saving mother is through enjoying life if I had no chance of enjoying her life?

Promise isn't a name

I

When I administer the laughing gas,
I learn how to breathe. The walls swell.
Blood pools her mind and steals her source
of hearted electricity. Her timber conducted
and grew only to the stretch of two palms
as a bowl. My tears kissed her limbs.

II

My house couldn't home her. I lit a fire
in the garden instead, poked at it and fed
it with hay. The sky broke with the weight
of un-cried losses, and doused the ground
with salty deaths that starved the burn.

III

White firefly flitting
in a black jelly jar
with broken wings.

III

We clench our hands into fists,
punch the sonar screen
and crawl into the gape.

IV

You are already becoming the wind,
our fingers can't hold you
but we spread them open like Oak.

VI

A hard soul to save, yet endured
the needles. Home is not
injected with cries.

VII

My skin held her organs.
My body holds her ghost.

VIII

I knit memories for her, purl
five loops to hold my index
with a tiny fist of wool. Both
baby and grandmother threading
a blanket to wrap farmed land.

IX

The hills of my chest crystallise
in the milk drought. I have two
glaciers in my mountain.

X

I intend to plant her so her memory
can centre then root then heal the ground
like our roots grew to the centre of her
then pick her reminding leaves following
her little feet to my gravestone door.

The earth is a better womb

in the bloody mud
an ovate belly opens
the start of the split

a labour of cream nutted crown
too great to feed pigs or keep
dormant then splitting

like a headache pushing
and pushing off the loath crisp
skull to unwind a spinal cord

petiole uncurling into tadasana
to reach into a congruence of green
hands to wave out the grave

giving itself space to stretch
stemmed to command the Sun
photosynthesise these palms

with a stroke of ray to stretch xylem
girth to make a shade to make work
for chainsaws and man birds

This is not the time

neither the place
or member you are
looking for. Your debt
won't be settled here.
I am not ready
to middle womb
you to the afterlife.
I open the toddler's door.
Pastel mountains bite
the dark. I guard
the frame, turn to face
in with half moon eyes,
say again *I am not ready*
you are not welcome here.
This is not the time for me
neither the place or member
you need to mediate
dimensions, to move you on.
A dress of breath wafts
sheer through me
I chase it
to the front door,
try to overtake through it
to open - to let them out.
Eyelashes blind out
just enough to hide
its white shadow.
I say out loud again

Come back. Come back.
I am not ready
I am not ready.
I didn't make it
to the door first.
The waft warmed up
in the hall, smoked
around the lightbulb,
exhaled in a dispersion
of atoms, as if separating
into tiny round planets,
imploding at my inability
to translate them, light-sped
off in many directions
to seek whoever it is they owe
to get them into heaven.

JOURNEY #2

As a child I'd felt at times a sense of a person stuck trying to find their way to the afterlife. They're trying to find a medium to channel and decipher them. Often, it's simply fear in the form of creaks or footsteps or a long breath in my ear or a pull of the sheets as I sleep or a drop in temperature all of a sudden, but I'm too scared to medium and instead treat them kindly so they don't stick around. Both of my Nan's have ghost stories. My Mom's Mom Frances had a poltergeist. Things would fly off the fireplace, and I seem to remember, though I was very young, a banging that would come down the stairs and a dark figure sitting at the end of the bed. My Dad's mom used to speak to a man on the stairs of her home and once pulled up to Frances's house but wouldn't get out of the car or even walk up the driveway for the feels she got from it. I've felt closer to the spirit of the dead since losing her. We often look for signs our loved ones are still with us after death in the Vedic web of life, carried in the air we cannot see.

A blossom of shame

I said it was a miscarriage on the phone
fourth floor on my own at a hotel dressed up

as education I could not afford
the food I bought, I did not know

what pesto was, I couldn't cook
for one. I cut my fingers carrying

sacks of dinners for four people
for a week to the bus.

I lied. He knew I lied. He said *Murderer*.
I lied. He said   *Murderer*.

Mom said *It's your choice*.
I chose this tiny room.

Home was vinegar and oil. I chose
not to tend a tree. This room barely

fits a spliff in asda bedsheets.
I showered on the toilet,

bled into the bowl. He did
not know I owned my womb.

I woke up to a doctors face
wide with ironed white beds

as teeth, clam open the words,
   It's all done.

The one they forget

A well-groomed nurse asks if you died
your hair. You ask why. She says there are no

fingers. You ask why. A silent consultant zooms
between your legs. Deformity confirmed.

The silent consultant puts her finger
on your mouth when you scream and gives you

a DVD of the Rorschach with a heartbeat you carry.
You take some pills. Sleep for a trinity. People

check your piss till you start to bleed.
They did not say it would be laborious.

A scrubbed nurse the size of the sky
pushes an induction past your vulva.

You wet the sheet.
You writhe.
You apologise.

You have never broken water.

You try to hide as the yoke comes.

They ask if you want a footprint.

You may say yes, but I lied
and urged them to discharge
the used condom I became.

Prolapse

Your home fingers on the abductors
to avoid falling in raspberry slush
at the rocks of my feet.

What if it comes out of me
when I'm standing at the cooker
or I have a fifth labour on the yoga mat?

I reach for arms and baby gates
to tilt me upright. I shouldn't stand
accept on my head and walk on my hands

with my feet together in grounded prayer.
Your home may set toward the heart then
and cement there.

At the end of the mist I find

an empty shopping trolly and
a pair of laddered tights
suspended as a bridge
in the milky tinnitus air
to a white waiting room
and he's sitting there
between two pixelated ancestors
with his palms on his knees
like an old man in confession
he sips at the mist
and I try to make myself aware
cough
forgetting it's more startling
than a wave that might make him
uncomfortable if he realised
I've been watching him
when I ask
how did you get here
and he then
I'm sorry bab
and I dissociate as he waits
for her
with a road of mountains
carved in his forehead
I grab the trolly and tell him
I have to go shopping
then find my Dad's hand
steering me to the checkout.

JOURNEY #3
When I arrived at the hospital, I blacked out when they said I was 10 centimetres dilated at only 23 weeks. In the black I found myself here, as I've written it. Our dear friend Geoff had died only months before, and he was in this waiting room waiting for her. He did take her in the end, you'll read that later.

REFLECTION #1
Spirit, soul, consciousness, whatever you want to call it, I had no gas and air nor pain relief at this point. It's in all of us this ghost. I believe our minds create familiar ways to support our fear in light of death. I wouldn't say he was an angel, though one person has told me without knowing this story that she is with him. Ask anyone who witnessed someone's last breath or heard someone at the end of life say 'They're here for me' and feel your chi right then and tell me there is no spirit. Here, I find medicine. I had to write it to make it real, and I did so in a workshop run by Caroline Bird.

Knocking

Opening the door
was more than a push
on and on and on and on,
until a tear at the cusp of
      can't take it any more
on and on and on
hum and hum and hum
then a light
too white to be blue
shone in a circle on my head
out like a lighthouse
torched across a landscape
of faces
miles and miles and miles
of faces
waiting
looked to me
to bring it on and on and on
I saw the other side
in me humming and knocking
hum and hum and hum
knock and knock and knock
push and push and push
miles and miles and miles
until the Sun rose
thorny and fighting
and all the faces rejoiced
in their first experience
of love.

Pace-making in Gogh's Corridor of the Asylum

Sometimes I say suite without the delivery
as if I was attending my own wedding
and had to reorganise the table plan
to replace drop-outs with stand-ins.

Other times I call it a hotel room.
'otel womb? I'd respond *Yes,*
the first thing I did was write lists
after the ceremony back in the hotel suite.

My body was nesting a life
whilst processing the life's death,
and I was rehearsing being born again
under the threshold of home empty-handed.

I walked lists back in that hotel room
and back down the aisle to the room
with perspex cots, like this portal
between birth and promise,

an undocumented amount of walks,
our backs walking away from her
towards the delivery room.
After that last walk, the concierge

offered pain relief for my empty womb
and I said no because I was busy
with the table plan. Pete walked out
of the suite and back with a remote

after that last walk back to the ward
and I lay in arms on the bed like a baby;
the covers swaddled me on their own
without a turndown service.

Then he called the nurse with the remote
for relief because I couldn't find my baby
in the delivery suite once I finished the lists,
once the walks stopped, and the nurses knew

I wouldn't want to feel my heart.

There's no one answer

In the immediacy of her
afterlife, relief, at least no life
of oxygen tanks, and I could sleep

without guilt I may wake
to her ending. At last, no life
of days hung up on intravenous

poles like question marks,
no intruding strangers asking
that I knew better and could advise

as life-giver against professions of life-savers
I had questioned the life out of on if
they thought her alive.

Kept in the underwear drawer

Someone framed a picture
of four of her fingers
on the pad of my index.

Too tiny to comprehend
why doctors mend
two hands' worth of being

whose hand fits
inside a fingerprint.
With tubes thin

as wire they pierced
her trachea fierce
as a pit stop crew

to air her lungs,
and raced her young
birth off to confront

God in the chapel
of babies. Someone captured
my identity in her clasp

after her 72-hour life
ended in an ink blot on one side
of her mind.

The stethoscope, ovary shaped
on her breastplate
lied about her heart rate.

She had died
by the time
they handed her mine.

A procession

dove asleep in a glass box
fluffed on a broken egg arrives

nan said *I wasn't expecting that*

uncle then *Can I carry her*

mom *yes, be careful*

carried on the shoulders
of four men gliding
to a flower bed
they place the dove
on a wide branch
at the meadows centre

mom *Is that ok?*

priest *Please sit.*

They sit down to listen
to a concert of ascension.
The dove won't feed all of us.
A curtain curves around the bird.
Mom goes to collect the flowers.

Apparently you leave them there.

REFLECTION #2

My daughter's funeral was oddly gorgeous. It was very intimate. I wish I had a friend there, and we thought we would feel ok about Pete's brother not coming, but we really did miss him. It was held at this beautiful crematory in Harborne. When she arrived in a tiny white coffin, my Mom said, 'I wasn't expecting that' before holding me up with her arm around my waist. I don't know what we were expecting, but I wasn't expecting it to be beautiful after the shock that coffins are made for such tiny beings.

When it ended, I rose to take the flowers. I didn't know this wasn't done. I wanted to bring her home with me, and the flowers were the only way. It was a mistake because I then had to watch them die, just as my partner had watched her go while I waited for the doctors to explain why she was born so early when they had the time.

JOURNEY #4

I imagined the coffin as a dove and the flowers as a wild garden for her burial. It started out as my perception but I changed it as if she is telling you the story of her funeral. She is watching it from above.

Warm up

empty pill packet
in my dressing gown pocket
in case there's one left

Ghosts in my mouth

SCENE;
Imagine you are inside a mouth, sitting on the mountain of a
tongue, looking out. The teeth in the jaw are a city skyline.

Not even a month
had roughed into cells,
my body buffed

into Shepard's delight
set inside the city's mouth - *Momma*
not gonna cry out. Night

is the safest time to die.
I gotta stop the codeine someday.
No one realised

I cleared out the packets,
that I swallowed each
tablet to jacket the cold.

When you keep something,
does that make it yours,
even if it's only a thought?

I asked God why everyone
was in my phone as I watched
choirs in the quiet on my own.

The spirits drift
from the plaque of teething offices,
their gospel like wildfire.

There are no stars here.
One of those spirits
is my bleeding gums.

My dentist asks
if I know anyone else that can sing.
I give them a name and listen

for the smoke to fold over my head.
It's static makes me scratch my skin
I wasn't ready for the Sun.

I wasn't prepared
to rise this way.
I stripped the duvet

out from between my legs,
carried my invisible motherhood
as a worn-in stain,

went back
to trafficked screen time
with a baby in a vase on my windowsill.

Dismiss progress

Failing to ignite inspiration
from propaganda, I deflate
in your entertainment.

Slice then roll you on,
lined up like hooked carcass.
It is necessary, I am still

aching for a healing society.
I just pick up the light
and lose myself

in your entertainment
reduced to proving
my life is human

because it is relatable.
When we're contributing
nothing, love us then.

The only place left
to exist silently now
is the nature we once were.

By holding my breath I

sucker myself
to the place
I am
it doesn't matter
where next
what's stopping me
I couldn't say
it's the way
I learned to breathe
that unconscious
act of heart
that harsh air
that makes us
scream
that makes us
too loud
straight away
when born
I really feel it
when I pause
I really feel it
I really feel
the gallop
halt
to a canter
to a jolt
I really feel
I'm almost dead
have escaped

being seen
have come
into this silent
as a saddle horse
to train
as a statue
to observe
as clay
to beat
to smooth
to contain
the eye
of observation
who sculpt
out of spite
out of rebellion
to feel their impulses
to feel fear
they may create
a body
they may
create a chance
to change.

Rams head

the home inside my body
shape shifts into an asylum
shape shifts into candle wax
shape shifts into tax evasion
shape shifts into shaved skin
shape shifts into daddy issues
shape shifts into a bottle of lube
shape shifts into a nature reserve
shape shifts into an empty library
shape shifts into a breakfast show
shape shifts into the hand of God
shape shifts into missing children
shape shifts into a rabbit in a cage
shape shifts into the therapy room
shape shifts into a coffin for a baby
shape shifts into a fairytale wedding
shape shifts into a reservoir of blood
shape shifts into an empty coffee cup
shape shifts into a cleaning cupboard
shape shifts into a table of steel objects
shape shifts into an off-duty police officer
shape shifts into a sign outside parliament
shape shifts into blossom picked for pleasure
shape shifts into a mood-swing on an oak tree

shape shifts into anger management for boys

shape shifts into a swell of plastic carrier bags

shape shifts into a hard working Mom on coke

shape shifts into a silent family at a dinner table

shape shifts into a desperate prayer from an atheist

shape shifts into a description of passive aggression

shape shifts into an orchestra playing Claude Debussy

shape shifts into two people fucking in a car in the dark

shape shifts into an electric guitar signed by Eric Clapton

shape shifts into the view from the international space station

shape shifts into a montage of every naked woman hung in an art gallery

Up age creek

Lashes locked.
A cheap blind.
White skin breaks
thick pine needles
from inside,
I'm itchy as a nest
of wings. I scratch,
leave raised heat,
tea pearls chip
my lip paint.
I zip up the bags
that swallow my face,
cheeks avalanche,
jowls cushion my voice.
Pores hoard dirt,
witches' pube arrives.
Potions lie.
Tits sunk
in airless lungs.
Yummy muffin
tuck yourself in
Mom jeans, *please.*
Jerkless bum.
Shoulders crying
for the sun. I smell
harder than a wash
basket. My limping hair
doesn't know how
to walk on the wind.

When we go dancing

There's a group of men
holding a meeting in my womb.
I'm a made-up girl with a woman's body
holding the sink in the toilets of a nightclub.

I read a note in lipstick on the mirror that says
I'm sorry bab.

There is neon graffiti all over the walls.
I'm a shiny photo from a disposable camera.

My family sit in a circle of toilets behind me,
cooing over my dying daughter
to the dying heartbeat of a song.

I pirouette down the plughole,
leave my body in the mouths of the men.

A priest stirs in the neonatal department.

I'm baptised.

The incubators prism rainbows
like chapel windows
stained with virgin tears.

How is this our church darling?
What intervention were we cursed?
What last supper is this -

both mothers, one brother, one sister-in-law, one nurse, a
priest we don't know, one consultant, you, me, a miracle just
three days old, a baby, a dead friend with two dead grand-
parents waiting, his holy hands the font, our family a chorus,
the room full of hymn?

We sang the Hail Mary.
A strip of golden light set on the priest
as our past friend materialised in the ray.
Our daughter, risen, took his hand and they
walked out down the nave.

No one knelt.

A moonrise darkened the room.
We followed her walk and I looked in your eyes,
swam through their salt, came to on the dance floor,
my back sweat greasing the palms of my girls.

Every morning I want to sleep forever,

my drumsticks won't move.

Every morning,
this robe
with cold feet
hoods my face like
a puddle in a sleep dent.

Every morning
I repeat the bucket list,
set unreachable targets
peel a smile wide teeth
to grit the screaming.

Every morning
my eyelids resist the light.

*Shut the fuck up,
it's warm in this bed.*

A ship for the animals

I hear
the end
gold
calling
even
when
I do
not ask,
its voice runs off a flood. I catch it in the silence, to
apprehend what it sighs, but there is so much water.
I build
myself
into
an ark,
raft
myself
between
two islands
facing the sky,
as an emblem
for Easter.

JOURNEY #5

This is one of my first expressions of spirituality in poetry. It's about 12 years old this piece, but it's been a work in progress all that time. I shared it with a friend before I edited it, and he didn't know what the 'gold' was. When I told him it's me trying to make sense of my thoughts, that I see a poem forming on the horizon. I'm trying to catch the gold of that. He just said 'oh' and it really knocked my confidence.

I left it for a long time until I came to put this collection together. It makes sense in the series of poems, this in-between being of birth and daughter and mother and woman. So, I completely stripped it, killed my darlings and made a cross because it represents my body in the poem as I float to find peace, to tune into my own advice. It's also a homage to my Irish Catholic ancestry though I only realised this writing this very reflection/journey. Maybe the voice of reason is God. Maybe the Sun is the original God and all religions are a metaphor. Maybe I'm too naive and have a whole lifetime of learning before I make such huge claims. Regardless, I hear the end gold calling, and when the rays hit me a poem is born.

I used to like the cage

with both gates closed;
no drafts, low lights,
punched cotton cushions
a box of emotions
on a magic carpet
chewing comfort
with a belly full of junk.

Now I can't stand
the lounging square
with both gates opened;
gusting breaths, highlights,
one limp cushion as a food tray
a microwaved coffee
a box of old tapes
hammock'ed in a springless daybed
with a scrambled brain
of spicy eggs.

.

Sneakerette

SCENE: Having a crafty fag out the bathroom window.

this thin rolled slice of smoke
sneaks in;
a beat of breath that blows me out;
a meditation before the advert of wellness;
an orgasm dessert;
a cough in a prayer;
a wealthy cloud;
a fossil sigh;
a black dog;
a rotten incense;
a fiery ash of grief;
a campfire in the city;
a fight with death;
a ray of war;
a ring of fire June wrote for Cash;
a sun tattoo in my eye;
a lift to nowhere;
a hug from me for myself in the cold;
pollen from a lily tarred on my id;
a stick of time;
a spray of old spice;
an air guitar;
a deep dick;
burnt speech;
some cheap therapy.

.

JOURNEY #6

When I watched the biopic Walk the Line, I found out June Carter wrote Ring of Fire and felt my entire body trying to communicate it was the women who found fire, and I took this as a stupid reason to continue smoking for a while feeling that burn and remembering with every light that a woman wrote a song I thought a man had written and women (maybe) found fire. Addicts find reasons to carry on chasing death, anxiety was mine.

Sometimes I can wash the day off

The slippery day
sleazy on my skin
drags to the shower,
takes two washes
in hot soap
with a thorough fist
in a hessian glove
to rub the people off
the morning after.
I scratch knots in my hair
it's good
at getting under my nails,
comb palm oil through.
Repeat.
Another abrasion drains off.
Sometimes I just stand there
for 28 minutes to reveal
the delicacy of my first kiss
when I'm scoured pink.
If the night
has lost some weight
I can wash the day off then.
If it does, I shake the duvet
slide in, rejuvenated.

Being like a mountain

Unzip me inside out.
Leave the planting
a little longer.

Each hand in search
undoes each knot
with fondness. Answer

the barren whistles
of this stripped bed,
unravel the object

undressed, unbrand us
into reason.
Skin on bark, pause speak

and hold on
with fondness. Answer
the fallen.

Unfold the pressure
of passion, pull me in this
stolen morning.

Those steep hills urge
our gasp outside, but here
is the view they stage.

Let's remind our bodies
to love, to lay
beside each want.

Hippy Crack

those silver bullets cocked on curbs and gravelled parks turn
teenagers into wolves in cars down backstreets in the night in
cities on summer afternoons at day raves on borrowed farm-
land after afters at the dawn and starve the brain mindless
when they learn the mindful give and take of breathwork
puckered on rubber lungs blown up with nos cracked in cream
canisters

they close their eyes to concentrate

breathe in eight beats   and hold it
blow slowly in the lung

and

back in again   and hold it

blow slowly out   until their lungs are emptied

and in eight beats   and hold it

blow slowly out

and there it is

and they forget who
they are and all thats left is corridors of breathing hexagons
they run through centres of mandalas and end up with two
numbers or two figures or two members of each sex with
multiple genders and two digits again of such satisfaction they
stop inhaling as they feel they've just figured out what reality
is and peace sets in as if they have the answers for why we exist
and there it is when they empty their lungs of silver gas and air
there it is the first breath before the first cry their heart flickers
and they resist until it threatens to blow out as the oxygen fades
its gone its gone its going they know when they hear sounds
stuttering back to collect and deliver them back to the park
to the backstreet to the farmland to the afters and the answer
dies once they inhale without the rubber lung I'd mastered
the give and take of breathwork for surges in gas masks and
the answers left me confusing the two dates of birth and
death and forever remembering her birthday the day she left

Head of curls

Everything you read here is a true mirage
and I was there all day in the hour long meditation.

It's one year since your daughter died.

A shaman drums on deer skin
over women on their backs
in a warehouse on a Digbeth backstreet
with sage smudging the eyelids.

The first landscape is neck-high
in wildflowers, sunlight reflecting
off the lens of an Arian child's eye.
At the edge, giant Sequoia's

picket gate a woodland of potential
spirit guides. You squeeze through
two trunks toward a cork oak
carved with a woman's face. You

laugh at yourself. Of course,
this is a projection of Grandmother
Willow that has nothing to do
with the drum you no longer hear

and you sit cupping laughter
head in hands with your back
against the bark and fall
in reverse between roots and land

in a rabbit's warren. Your hands
sink into the earth and you drown
through the ground into a quartz
cave. You crawl through its mouth

and root regurgitated on meadow
foxtail. There is no skyward ocean.
Teenage wildflowers gossip
as a boar comes forward

Are you my spirit guide?
it snuffs at the air. You follow
them into the redwood city.
A Common Blue comes

Are you my spirit guide?
and it flutters unimaginatively
to a fawn. *You are the drum
in the roof of this sky* and it bows

to a white horse in a circle of light.
What does it all mean?
You stroke his mane knowing full well
it's manufactured for the princess

your Dad called you. It guides
you to a pool of petrol, like a giant
vinyl. At the centre, a drip of white light.
A boat arrives. You row toward the drip.

She is stood there, hip high
on a rock like a Selkie. You expect
to run right through her
but you hold her so hard she could

grow in you again. You mirage
a cake, eat crustless sandwiches, pour
tea, swing her, dip her toes in the black
sea and celebrate her birthday.

Don't use the guest towels

The shore is uncertain.
It misses the tide, and thinks
too much of its return.

Most of the time I prepare
my shell; sense it pressed
on the wind's window

like a child as I wash.
Apart from keeping you
at bay, I wear the breeze

of your fingers,
that tide-long travelling
tosses me before it returns.

To be captain

it will meet you now
 in a room
  with a draft
   down the hall
    where a bike leans
     on your plate
      a rogue strand
       of foreign hair
        at the party
         it will greet you
          wearing feathers
           and a frown
            and when it tries to
             kiss your hand
              you will act surprised
               and let us know
                you hate surprises
                 either way love,
                  the choreography
                   of staging
                    the family portrait
                     will stain a square
                      on the wallpaper
                       when you leave.

REFLECTION#3

I find people's anxieties around social events tend to come true.

If you're going to worry, and everyone is telling you not to, you will want your imagined problems to come true so you can say, 'I told you so'. You'll also look for said problems at the event, even if you're trying to have a good time, just to prove to yourself it is worth the worrying. By constantly thinking up problems, I believe we manifest them into reality. Our perceptions become just that, a vision of worry. There is a comfort in this for the worrier I haven't quite figured out through the little psychology I've studied.

I did this. I blamed myself for failing to carry her full term as if I was in control of my own body. In waiting for problems, in worrying about money, I took on too much and was busy and heavy with the weight of expectation and provision. Had I known I had an incompetent cervix, I'd have taken bed rest as fundamental for her incubation - had I had the peace and confidence I could provide without working myself into oblivion, I may not have gone into labour.

Of course, all of this is bullshit. It's 'isness', it just is. Seven years on I am still worrying about stuff I know nothing of.

JOURNEY #7
I wanted the poem to feel like you're falling down the stairs to create the nervous anxiety you get in social situations, hence the positioning of the lines.

On life being life because love

There are many loves in this life
which is why it's so hard to find love

in this life. Though this life
split itself, avid to love, love

focused on multiplying this life,
positioning itself as a collection of loves

but, love isn't collectible as life
says love is; you cannot focus on love

multiplying, love is more like life
stories tell us love isn't, that's the love

adjusted to life. The many words life
tries to communicate love, make love

unheard of. Poems articulating life
aren't the love life's interested in. Love

has no language. It's so close to live and life
'o' replaces 'i' to confuse this life with love

round, like a year, like a planet, like life
or a kiss that cannot kiss itself to love

itself with love. Love can't just be life
it's too simple and anyway, whole loves

are lost in land destroyed by life
at a loss with itself with the idea love

is collectible, like land, like things, like life
collects lives to contain or erase love

in the name of love, to liberate life
defining love as anything other than love.

Immaculate

In the living room in the heart
I hold in my hand, you and I
are dancing to Madonna.

When I think of you, I see
the *M* for Mom in Madge's cover
on her Immaculate Collection;

Cherish, Vogue, Lucky Star,
Like a Virgin, Express yourself
on the telly vision, your voice

rings blood through my ears,
our hip pirouettes in slow motion
like artistic swimmers as the Sun

pours through the bay window.
As I catch my breath, Cerutti
and Bristow choke me

when you whip your perm.
When I think of your voice
it lays a road to the 90s, and

when I think of us I wish
it's always this on a Saturday
morning you teaching me

what adulthood should be -
wrapped in fishnet, karaoke
and rosary beads with a vacuum

for a microphone and someone to dance with.

Yin Yang Hounds

One night, I came down a hill in oversized sky-blue linen.
I am four or five sizes bigger in this dream with a straw sunhat

in the Lagos sun, my skin the shade of Roma, my adoptive grandmother,
my lips nude in suncream. I came to the barn with a bucket of seed,

followed by two huge dogs coming at me fast, one white, one black.
The white one went past, and I had to hold my hat. I turned

on his whip to greet the black dog jump at my throat, and it bit
into the right side of my neck, right under my ear, into my voice.

I thought I'd stop smoking after that dream. I even told Jenny
it was a sign from some version of me I might become, but

I didn't stop then; I only did when Betty came down with it
in her breast. Now I read about the black dog of depression

as I study the counselling section of my degree and wonder
if the yang of the two dogs was the cancer I believed

it warned or a decree of the human need to depress in the justice
of understanding. Since then, there's a tone in my ear I can't turn off.

It was a static you could confuse with a crowd, but now it's a tone
from a singing bowl too. I hear it most in the quiet though

I do get aggressive when there's too many frequencies; I become
that black dog sewing itself to my throat with its moonshine teeth.

I think of her when I hear the piano

I hear a note.
I hear the moon,
the night cloud's lifting.

This gift arrives
and closes my curtains.
I sink into pensive cushions.

Her fingers couldn't play.

I think about us meeting again.
He told me she's just
trying to find her way back.

Sure, there's a body with
her in it queuing with her mates
in the dark, laughing for real
at a shit joke, testing
someone's patience.

She's out there, living in that
moment of sound.

One singular note of a piano
reflecting off adolescent mirrors.

Now and then

A tight feast before,
not fluffed to pillow a whole human,
could nest a man's head,
would leave a mouth wet
couldn't conjure antibodies,
no vitamins to share,
no gold fountain came,
I was just a wrack of nips and flesh.

A supple bounce now,
alive and lived in.
A bottle of nectar,
react to saliva,
two cups of silk honey
pumped by tiny hands
holy and honoured
my veining breasts,
a gorge for a suckling
crown of lips.

Hail Mary, full of grace

I try to digest
the whole daughter
she always comes up in sons.
There's religion in my belly
which can't satisfy the daughters
regurgitating over and over and over and

ACKNOWLEDGEMENTS

Thanks to Pete for the sunflower seeds, for the boys, for the pursuits, for the encouragement. If you hadn't said you were going to publish them,

I wouldn't have published them.

Thanks to Stuart for asking the right questions, for the support, for the truth and most importantly, your patience.

Thanks to Cecilia for her confidence, analysis, editorial and direction.

Thanks to Nici for your tender grief work.

Thanks to Mom for all the heart padlock secret diaries.

Thanks to Mr Scott for teaching us poetry before our school became an academy.

Thanks to Uncle Darren for the handwritten poetry books.

Thanks to JP for reading all I had and finding her in a sequence that made this.

Thanks to Karen McCarthy Woolf, Rebecca Goss, Helen Calcutt and Wendy Pratt. Your vulnerability and honesty, your grief and expression let me feel and write from wanting to know feeling.

Thanks to Jonathan Davidson for asking why I wasn't writing like I read.

Thanks to Jenny for constantly reminding me 'you are an artist!'.

Thanks to Vicky for the hype and belief.

Thanks to Inès Elsa Delal for the crumbling, raw, breathless, passionate consistency.

Thanks to ACE.

Thanks to Birmingham Women's Hospital.

Thanks to *Wasaaaabi* for comparing me to both flora and terrier, for space, for peace, for openness, for form, for nonsense, for art, for poetry, for mornings, for coffee, for measure, for love.

ABOUT VERVE POETRY PRESS

Verve Poetry Press is a prize-winning press that focused initially on meeting a local need in Birmingham - a need for the vibrant poetry scene here in Brum to find a way to present itself to the poetry world via publication. Co-founded by Stuart Bartholomew and Amerah Saleh, it now publishes poets from all corners of the UK - poets that speak to the city's varied and energetic qualities and will contribute to its many poetic stories.

Added to this is a colourful pamphlet series, many featuring poets who have performed at our sister festival - and a poetry show series which captures the magic of longer poetry performance pieces by festival alumni such as Polarbear, Kevin P. Gilday and Imogen Stirling.

The press has been voted Most Innovative Publisher at the Saboteur Awards, and has won the Publisher's Award for Poetry Pamphlets at the Michael Marks Awards.

Like the festival, we strive to think about poetry in inclusive ways and embrace the multiplicity of approaches towards this glorious art.

www.vervepoetrypress.com
@VervePoetryPres
mail@vervepoetrypress.com